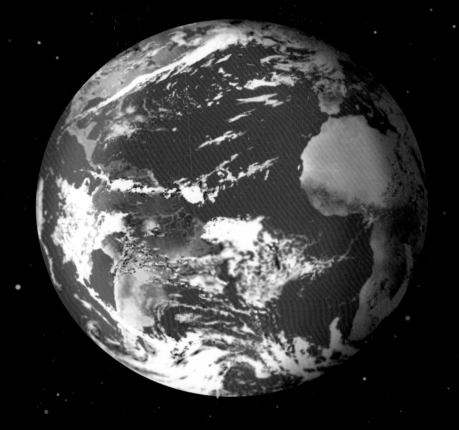

THE BOOK OF PLANET EARTH

THE BOOK OF PLANET EARTH

AUTHOR: Clint Twist
ILLUSTRATOR: Kuo Kang Chen
ART EDITOR: Duncan Brown
EDITOR: Elise See Tai
ART DIRECTOR: Miranda Kennedy
EDITORIAL MANAGER: Ruth Hooper
PRODUCTION DIRECTOR: Clive Sparling

Created and produced by Andromeda Children's Books
An imprint of Pinwheel Ltd
Winchester House
259–269 Old Marylebone Road
London NW1 5XJ, UK

ISBN-10: 1-86199-183-5
ISBN-13: 978-1-86199-183-6

9 8 7 6 5 4 3 2 1

Printed in Malaysia

CONTENTS

PLANET EARTH

We live on Earth, a planet that orbits a star called the *Sun*. When viewed from space, Earth looks like a blue-green ball. Huge oceans provide the blue color. The oceans surround large continents of land that are mostly covered by green plants. Earth is now a good place to live, with mild temperatures across most of its surface. It was not always like this.

MYTHS AND LEGENDS

The ancient Sumerians, who once lived in southern Iraq, believed that the Earth was shaped like a huge flat plate covered by an upside-down bowl that was the sky. They thought that both the Earth and the sky were carried on the back of a giant turtle swimming through an ocean.

FACTS AND FIGURES

DIAMETER: 7,926 miles (12,756 km)
DISTANCE FROM SUN: 93 million miles (150 million km)
AVERAGE SURFACE TEMPERATURE: 59°F (15°C)
TIME TAKEN TO ORBIT THE SUN: 365.25 days

MYTHS AND LEGENDS

The Viking seafarers who raided throughout Europe during the Middle Ages had their own views on the origin of the Earth. They believed that the land of rock and water—the world they inhabited—was created as the result of a great battle between the land of ice and the land of fire.

FORMATION

COLLISION

About 4.4 billion years ago, before the Earth was fully formed, it collided with a large planetismal. The impact blasted a lot of material from Earth's surface into space. Gradually, this material came together to form the Moon—a natural satellite that orbits the Earth about once a month. After the Moon formed, it did not develop in the same way as the Earth. The Moon has a bare, empty surface with no water and no plants—just dry dust and bare rock.

MYTHS AND LEGENDS

In Finland, people once believed that the Moon was one of six golden eggs laid by a wild duck in the lap of a sleeping girl made from air. When the girl woke up, she stood up and scattered the eggs, which smashed into the sea. One of the eggs became the Moon, while the others became the Sun, the stars, and the clouds.

FACTS AND FIGURES

THE MOON:
DIAMETER: 2,160 miles (3,476 km)
DISTANCE FROM EARTH: 252,697 miles (406,676 km)
AVERAGE SURFACE TEMPERATURE: 1.4°F (-17°C)
TIME TAKEN TO ORBIT THE EARTH: 29.5 days

COLLISION

BOMBARDMENT

The Earth was a hot and dangerous place about 4 billion years ago. Although the surface was cooled by the cold of space, there was still plenty of heat below Earth's surface. Streams of hot liquid rock from inside the Earth poured out of cracks and volcanoes to the surface. Not all the lumps of material in the original dust cloud had formed into planetismals and planets. Many lumps were still speeding through space as meteorites. For hundreds of millions of years, meteorites bombarded the Earth. This bombardment stopped about 3.5 billion years ago. Some small meteorites still hit Earth every year.

MYTHS AND LEGENDS

Meteorites often make a bright streak of light, called a *meteor*, in the night sky when they burn up in Earth's atmosphere. The ancient Greeks believed that meteors were thunderbolts hurled by the god Zeus. This belief would have been strengthened if they had found pieces of meteorite after seeing the meteor blaze through the sky.

LOOKING CLOSER

Located in the Painted Desert region of Arizona, Meteor Crater is a massive circular hole about 39,000 feet (12,000 m) across and about 575 feet (175 m) deep. It formed about 50,000 years ago when a 165-foot (50-m) meteorite crashed into the ground at 40,000 mph (65,000 km/h).

BOMBARDMENT

MYTHS AND LEGENDS

Some ancient North American people believed that the Earth's dry land was made from mud or sand brought up from beneath the ocean by an animal. The Mandan people believed that a wild duck dived down to the ocean bed. According to the Cherokee people, the animal was a water beetle named *Beaver's Grandchild*.

FACTS AND FIGURES

Earth's present-day atmosphere consists of the following gases:

NITROGEN: 78%
OXYGEN: 21%
ARGON: 0.95%
CARON DIOXIDE, HELIUM, NEON, AND OTHER GASES: 0.05%

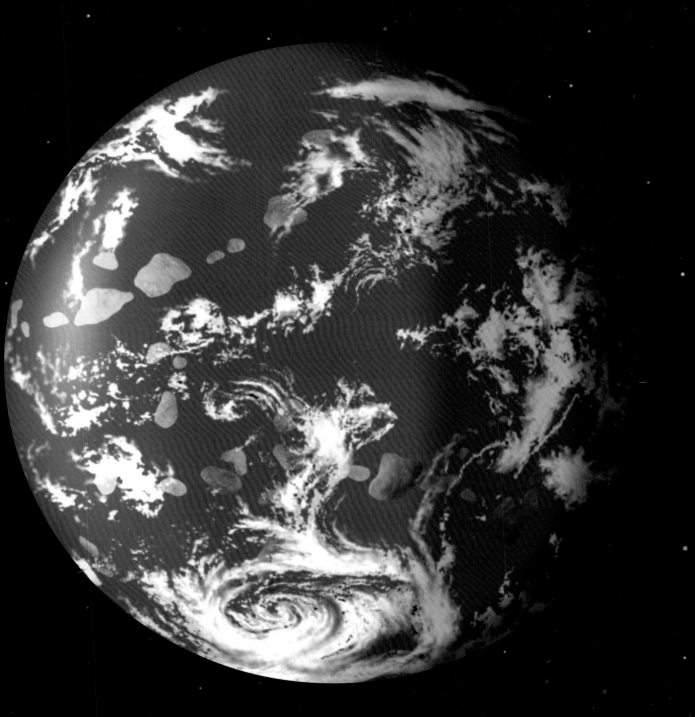

SNOWBALL

About 700 million years ago, Earth became so cold that all the land was covered beneath snow and ice. The oceans nearly froze over completely. The only unfrozen parts were a few small patches of open water in the warmest parts of the Earth around the equator. Tiny plants continued to live in the ocean underneath the ice. By this time, there were tiny animals as well. When conditions became warmer and "Snowball Earth" thawed out, some animals in the ocean became larger and more complicated. Jellyfish and worms were among the first of these larger animals. About 550 million years ago, the first animals with eyes and jointed legs began living in shallow waters.

MYTHS AND LEGENDS

It is much easier to imagine a land covered in ice if you live in a cold climate. In Norway, people once believed in a land of ice called *Niflheim*. It was inhabited by huge frost-giants that were the enemies of the Norwegian gods.

LOOKING CLOSER

The appearance of animals with eyes and legs about 550 million years ago is often called the *Cambrian Explosion*—an explosion of life. Earth's history since that time has been divided into a series of named periods, each lasting for tens of millions of years. The first of these, the *Cambrian period*, began about 545 million years ago.

tinents was clumped
continent, called
gea was filled with
fish with bony
thousands of plants,
ch as amphibians,
s. Pangea stayed
on years. Afterward,
nto our modern-

MYTHS AND LEGENDS

Native Australians believed that long ago there was *Dreamtime*. In Dreamtime, all the animals were asleep under the Earth and nothing happened on the surface. Present-day life began when Dreamtime ended— all the animals woke up and dug their way to the surface.

LOOKING CLOSER

The Earth's solid surface (crust) is divided into a series of plates that "float" on the semi-liquid rock beneath. Powered by heat currents from deep within the Earth, these plates gradully shift position over millions of years. This process is called *plate tectonics*.

IMPACT

Meteorites are not the only things left over from the formation of the planets. There are thousands of much larger objects that are known as *asteroids*. Some asteroids are more than 60 miles (100 km) across, although most are smaller. Earth gets hit by one of these asteroids about once every 100 million years. The last time this happened was 65 million years ago, when an asteroid about 6 miles (10 km) in diameter smashed into the Earth. The impact caused a huge explosion and made a crater more than 240 miles (400 km) wide. The heat of the explosion and the huge quantities of dirt blown into the atmosphere caused an environmental catastrophe. It is estimated that about three quarters of all animal species died, including the land-living dinosaurs.

MYTHS AND LEGENDS

In ancient Mexico, people believed there had once been a terrible Earth-monster named *Tlaltecuhtli*. This monster was a cross between a giant toad and a crocodile, with fangs and long claws. Tlaltecuhtli also had extra mouths on its elbows and knees. It was known as the "Lord of Earth."

LOOKING CLOSER

The crater made by the asteroid 65 million years ago is now hidden beneath the seabed in the Gulf of Mexico. Scientists discovered proof of the asteroid's effect on Earth when they found a thin layer of iridium-rich clay in 65-million-year-old rock in different parts of the world. Iridium is a metal that is very rare on Earth, but is quite common in meteorites and asteroids.

was cold enough for
rts of America, Europe,
at present. During the
0 years ago, a layer of ice
hed as far south as the
ndon, England. The Ice
rs ago. After the ice
rvived the cold began
ere especially good.
and pottery and
wns.

MYTHS AND LEGENDS

In the Andes Mountains of South America, ancient peoples believed that everything had been made by Pachacamac the Creator. When Pachacamac made the first people, they soon starved to death from lack of food. Pachacamac then made some more people, but this time he showed them how to grow corn, fruit, and vegetables so they could feed themselves.

FACTS AND FIGURES

Since the invention of farming, the
human population of the Earth has
increased dramatically.

DATE	POPULATION
10,000 BC	5 million
100 BC	100 million
AD 1000	300 million
AD 1500	450 million
AD 1800	900 million
AD 1900	1.6 billion
AD 2000	6 billion

EARTH'S LAYERS

The center of the Earth, called the *core*, is a white-hot ball of nearly pure metal (a mixture of iron and nickel). Surrounding the core is the *mantle*, a thick layer of semi-solid rock known as *magma*. The outer surface layer, called the *crust*, is very thin compared to the mantle. The thickest parts of the crust are under the continents, while the thinnest crust is under the oceans.

FACTS AND FIGURES

Earth's core is about 4,200 miles (6,800 km) in diameter. Earth's mantle is about 1,800 miles (2,900 km) thick. Earth's crust varies from 1 to 45 miles (1–75 km) thick.

VOLCANOES

Magma in the mantle is kept semi-liquid by the pressure of the rock above, but when it escapes onto the surface, it flows across the surface as lava. The escape of magma from the mantle is known as *volcanic activity*.

MID-OCEAN RIDGES

The most important volcanic activity is hidden from view on the ocean bed. New crust is created when magma escapes through long cracks in the ocean floor, creating a ridge in mid-ocean and pushing the existing crust outward. The mid-Atlantic ridge is making the Atlantic Ocean wider at a rate of about ½ inch (1 cm) per year—this is about as fast as your fingernails grow.

SUBDUCTION ZONES

At the edges of the oceans, the volcanic activity in mid-ocean forces the thinner ocean crust beneath the thicker crust of the continents. This process, which is

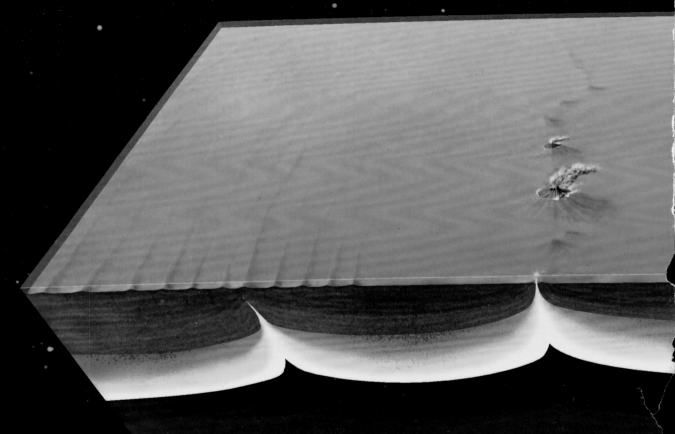

THE ATMOSPHERE

Earth's atmosphere extends 310 miles
(500 km) from its surface. Most of the
air we breathe is concentrated at the
bottom of the atmosphere in the
lowest 16,000 feet (5,000 m). The
atmosphere protects life on Earth in
a number of different ways. It burns
up thousands of meteorites each year.
The atmosphere also filters out a lot of
harmful radiation from space. A high-
level ozone layer screens out most of
the dangerous ultraviolet (UV) light
in sunlight. The atmosphere also acts
like an insulating blanket, allowing
the Earth to retain much of the heat
energy it receives from the Sun.

FACTS AND FIGURES

The atmosphere is divided into layers:

LAYER	HEIGHT ABOVE SURFACE
TROPOSPHERE	0–6 miles (0–10 km)
STRATOSPHERE	6–30 miles (10–50 km)
MESOSPHERE	30–50 miles (50–80 km)
THERMOSPHERE	50–310 miles (80–500 km)

26

SOLID SURFACE

There are three types
of rock in the crust.
SEDIMENTARY: rocks
such as sandstone and
limestone that were
laid down in layers.

IGNEOUS: rocks such
as granite and basalt
are magma that has
erupted through the
crust from the mantle
and become solid.

METAMORPHIC: rocks such
as marble and slate that
have been changed by the
heat of nearby magma.
Marble is limestone
that has been

transformed by heat
inside the Earth.

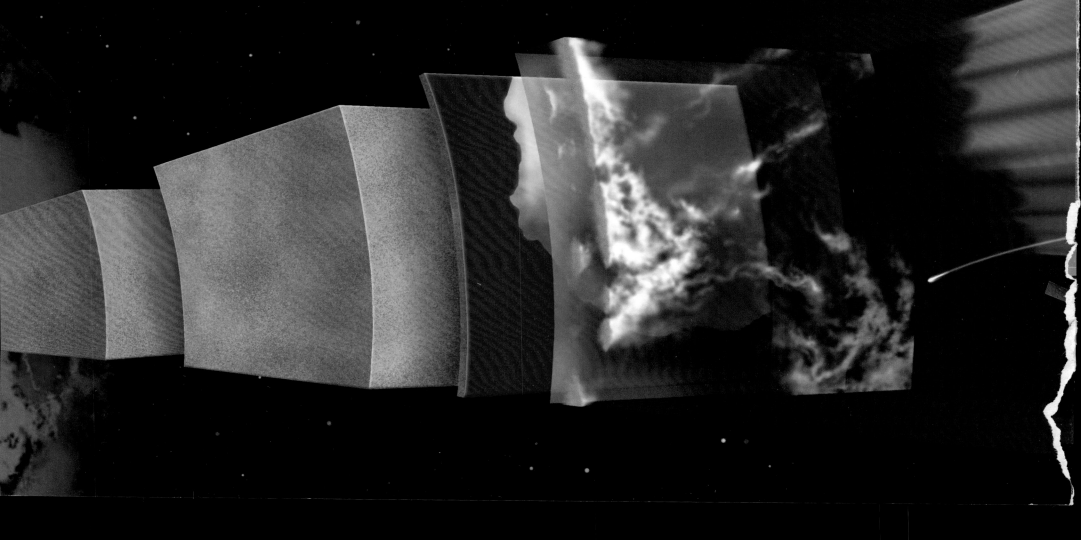

known as *subduction*, often causes
volcanoes to erupt on the land above.
The most famous example is the *Ring of
Fire* that surrounds the Pacific Ocean.

VOLCANIC CONES

A typical volcano is cone-shaped. Each time the volcano
erupts, layers of larva and ash build up, making the cone
bigger. Erupting volcanoes are described as *active*, volcanoes
that are between eruptions are *dormant*, and volcanoes that
have not erupted for a long time are *extinct*.

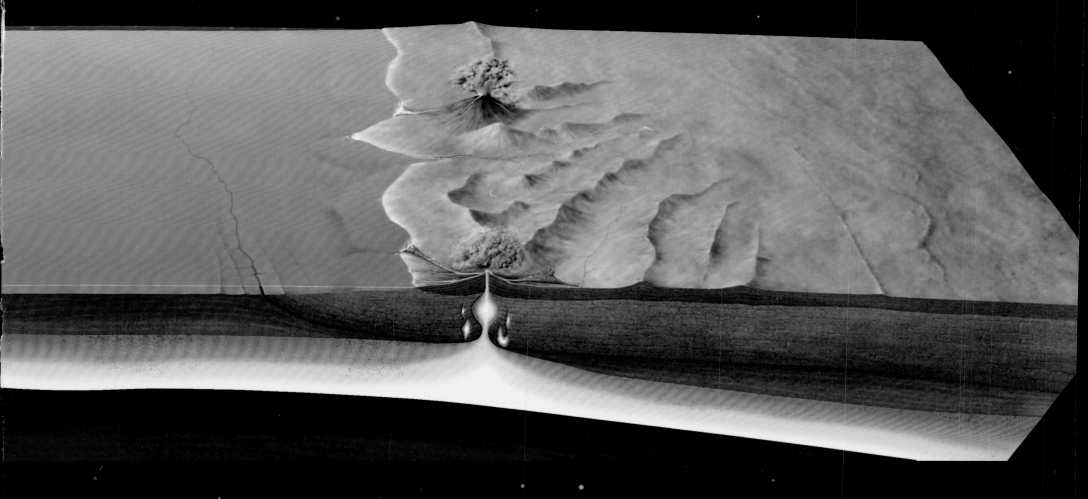

GLOSSARY

ASTEROID
A large chunk of rock that orbits the Sun.

ATMOSPHERE
A layer of gas surrounding a planet. Earth's atmosphere consists mainly of nitrogen and oxygen.

CLIMATE
The average yearly pattern of weather in a particular place.

CONTINENT
A large area of land surrounded by oceans.

CRATER
A roughly circular depression in a planet's surface, often surrounded by steep cliffs, caused by a high-speed impact.

CRUST
The solid outer surface of a planet that is made from rock.

EQUATOR
A line drawn on maps and globes that is midway between the North Pole and the South Pole.

ICE AGE
A time in the past when Earth's climate was colder than at present.

MANTLE
A thick layer of hot, semi-liquid rock inside the Earth.

METEORITE
One of millions of small chunks of rock that travel through space.

ORBIT
To travel through space around a planet or star; the path through space made by an orbiting object.

PANGEA
A super-continent that began to break up about 250 million years ago.

PLANET
A large spherical object that orbits a star.

PLANETISMAL
A large mass of rock that existed during the formation of the solar system.

SATELLITE
An object that orbits a planet.

SNOWBALL
The name given to a planet that is completely covered with snow and ice.

STAR
A huge, spinning ball of hot gas in space with a maximum size of more than 6 million miles (10 million km) in diameter.

SUN
The nearest star to Earth and the center of the solar system.

INDEX